Hophead Harry

Goes to the Brewery

Written by Dennis Kistner

Illustrated by Beth-Ann Wilson

Hophead Harry Goes to the Brewery

Copyright © 2016 by Dennis Kistner

Illustrated by Beth-Ann Wilson

Designed and edited by Chandler Vicchio

Library of Congress
Cataloging in Publication Data

ISBN 978-0-692-73920-4

Proudly manufactured in the United States of America

Bubs Publishing

Baltimore, MD

For my wife, son, family, and friends
Thanks for everything

Hello. Hophead Harry here.

Come meet my friends,
and we'll learn how to make beer.

First, I'll show you the farm, my home,

where hops like me
are planted and grown.

1

These are called hop vines;

they grow in the sun.

We will add them to beer

before we are done.

Cone-shaped buds are called hops;

they are bitter and strong.

We have to get them to the brewery.

We can't take too long!

We'll put the hops in bags

and load them in a van.

Then we will meet Bobby Barley,

if things go as planned.

3

Here is Bobby Barley. He's a great friend of mine.

Barley is a kind of grain, like in your toast at breakfast time.

Barley starts as a plant in the ground right here,

but it must become malt to be turned into beer.

Let's go meet Mary Malts; she's part of our crew.

Then it's off to the brewery to make some craft brew!

Look! Over there,

it's Mary Malts standing by her house.

She's wearing cowgirl boots
and a pretty pink blouse.

Howdy, y'all. I'm really glad that we could meet.

I look like Bobby Barley—just cuter and sweet.

Malting makes barley easy to use.

Soon we'll meet Brewmaster Brooks and make some yummy brews.

Now it is time to get packed and loaded, safe and sound.

Then we'll all leave in the delivery truck and go to the brewery in town.

At the brewery, we'll meet Brewmaster Brooks;
it's not far from here.
He'll take all of the ingredients
and make some great craft beer.

Welcome to the brewery, everyone.

It's time to learn about beer and have some fun.

I'm Brewmaster Brooks, and I brew beer

from all of the ingredients we have right here.

Now let's go inside, and we can start to brew.

Just follow me around, and I'll show you what to do.

11

These tanks and pipes are all used to make beer.

The time to start brewing is almost here.

It's Brewmaster Brooks and Wendy Water
by that tank labeled 'Mash Tun.'

MASH TUN

The first step in the process has just begun.

I wash the grains in these tanks that are silver and large.

This is the next step of brewing, and it is called the sparge.

From the sparge comes wort; it is sugary, hot, and sticky.

It has to be just right because we brewmasters are very picky.

Brewmaster Brooks pumps the wort
into a big brew kettle.

It's another tank in the brewery
also made of metal.

Now the wort is heated until it is boiling hot.

Hops are added to the wort—sometimes a little, sometimes a lot.

The bitter hops help balance the wort, which is sweet and sugary.

Balanced with sweet malt and bitter hop—
that's how great beer should be.

After the wort and hops are boiled,
   it is time for liquid to cool down.

Brewmaster Brooks pumps the fluid into the fermenter,
   which is big, silver, and round.

17

When the wort is the right temperature, Brewmaster Brooks adds yeast.
They are tiny living things, and on the wort's sugar they will feast.

As the yeast eat, thrive, and grow, they turn the wort into finished beer.

This process can take a few weeks and happens in these tanks right here.

After all of our hard work,
there's not much left to do.

We are almost finished
with our freshly made craft brew.

It is time to drain our beer
into kegs and cans.

Then we will load them into trucks as quickly as we can.

Once the trucks are loaded up as carefully as can be,
the beer is off to the local pub to be enjoyed responsibly.
Thanks for helping us at the brewery; we hope you had fun.

Now you know how brewing
craft beer is done!

23

CPSIA information can be obtained at www.ICGtesting.com
Printed in the USA
BVIW12n0001200916

462510BV00020B/11